Contents

Introduction	5
Excavator	6–7
Site dumper	8
Rock breaker	9
Bulldozer	10
Handheld breaker	11
Tipper truck	12
Loader	13
Backhoe loader	14–15
Tracked dumper	16
Mini dumper	17
Demolition excavator	18
High tip dumper	19
Skid steer loader	20
Articulated dump truck	21
Auger drill	22
Heavy tipper truck	23
Mass excavator	24–25
Waste handler	26
Refuse compactor	27

Mini excavator 28

Dragline excavator 29

Tractor loader 30

Trencher 31

Semi-trailer dump truck 32–33

Heavy hauler dump truck 34

Electric rope shovel 35

Transfer dump truck 36

Scraper 37

Grader 38–39

Telehandler 40

Useful words 41

Spotter's guide 42-47

Find out more 48

Digger and dumper safety

Diggers and dumpers are powerful machines. They can be very dangerous. Always have an adult with you when you look at diggers, dumpers, and other machines. Do not stand near diggers and dumpers. Never touch a digger or dumper. Never walk or play on a building site.

Diggers and dumpers

Diggers and dumpers are machines that help to get jobs done. Some machines dig, lift, or crush. Others carry materials from place to place. Look out for busy excavators and loaders. Listen for the noise of dumpers tipping out their loads.

You can spot diggers and dumpers on building sites, farms, and travelling or working on roads. This book will help you to name the diggers and dumpers you see.

At the back of this book is a Spotter's Guide to help you remember the diggers and dumpers you find. Tick them off as you spot them. You can also find out the meaning of some useful words here.

Turn the page to find out all about diggers and dumpers!

Excavator

Excavators are digging machines. The operator moves the arm to scoop up bucketfuls of soil and rubble.

Metal teeth help the bucket cut into the ground.

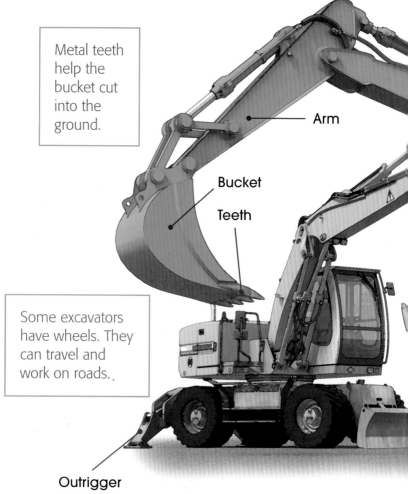

Arm

Bucket

Teeth

Some excavators have wheels. They can travel and work on roads.

Outrigger

The platform turns from side to side to dump the load.

Boom

Crawler tracks help this excavator travel across rough or muddy ground without slipping or sinking.

Controls

Driver's cab

Turntable

Counterweight

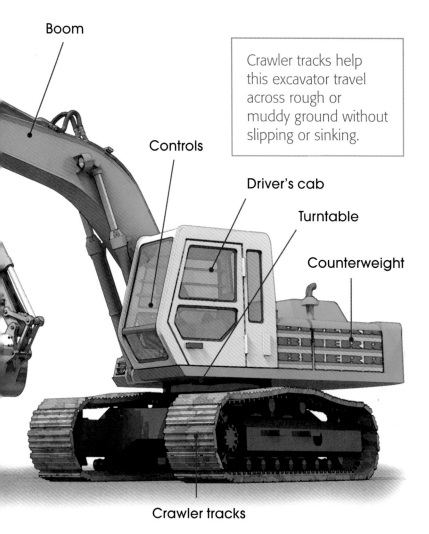

Crawler tracks

Site dumper

Dumpers carry heavy loads around building sites. The operator pushes a button to tip the skip forwards and dump the load quickly.

This dumper can carry 7000 kg – the weight of more than 100 adults!

Warning light

Roll bar

Skip body

Rock breaker

Special tools can be bolted on to excavators to help them do different jobs. A rock breaker lets this excavator smash through hard ground.

The rock breaker works like a powerful hammer. It can break stone and concrete.

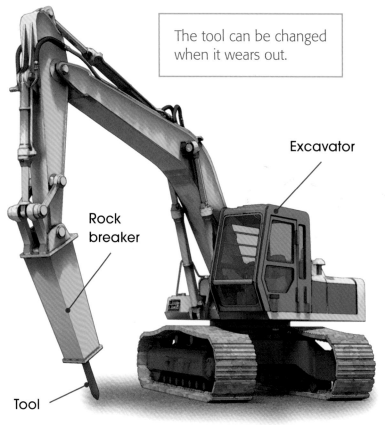

The tool can be changed when it wears out.

Excavator

Rock breaker

Tool

Bulldozer

Powerful bulldozers clear earth, rocks, and trees by pushing them out of the way. They can flatten huge areas of land quickly, ready for a road, railway, or building.

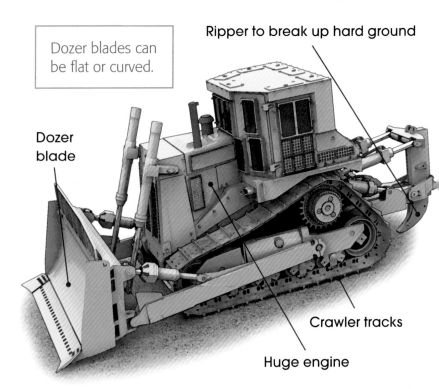

Dozer blades can be flat or curved.

Ripper to break up hard ground

Dozer blade

Crawler tracks

Huge engine

The blade's sharp edge scrapes across the ground.

Handheld breaker

Handheld breakers are used for small digging jobs, like digging through a road to mend a pipe. The tough steel tool can smash up hard ground or tarmac.

Ear protectors

Blasts of air push a piston down to hit the top of the tool. This hammers the tool against the ground many times each second.

Air goes in here

Tool

Tipper truck

Tipper trucks are lorries with a tipping cargo area. They can travel on roads. They can carry loads much further than dumpers.

Piston arms lift the front of the truck bed high into the air. The load slides out of the back.

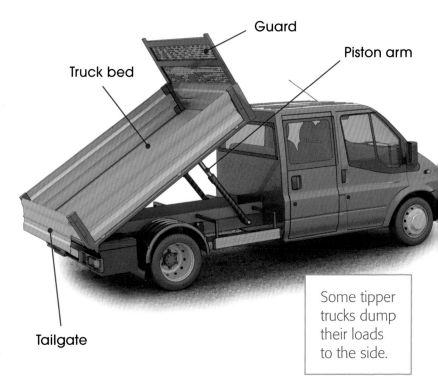

Guard

Piston arm

Truck bed

Tailgate

Some tipper trucks dump their loads to the side.

Loader

This machine scoops and lifts heavy loads. It can move sand around a building site, dig a hole, or load a truck with rubble.

The huge bucket scoops up large loads in one go. This helps to get a job done quickly.

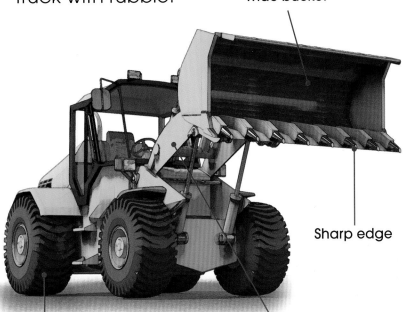

Wide bucket

Sharp edge

Large tyres

Arms to lift and lower bucket

Strong arms lift the bucket high above the ground.

Backhoe loader

This useful machine does many different jobs. The big bucket at the front scoops up rubble, flattens earth, and pushes things out of the way.

Cab

Arm to lift and lower bucket

Loader bucket

The long arm at
the back digs holes
and trenches.

Backhoe loaders are
used on building
sites everywhere.

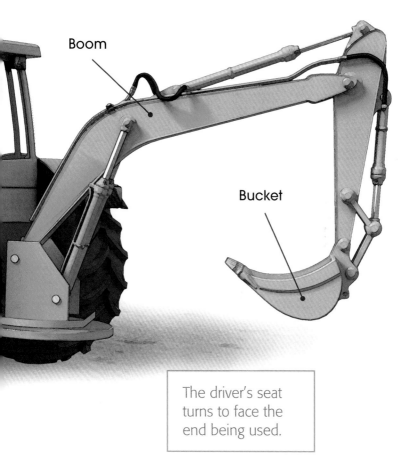

Boom

Bucket

The driver's seat
turns to face the
end being used.

Tracked dumper

Dumpers with tracks can work on rough or muddy ground. They can turn around in small spaces.

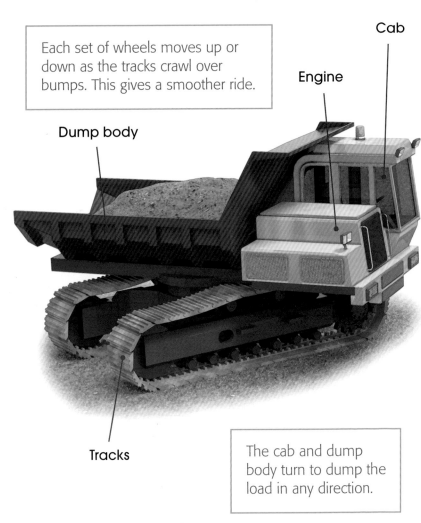

Each set of wheels moves up or down as the tracks crawl over bumps. This gives a smoother ride.

Cab

Engine

Dump body

Tracks

The cab and dump body turn to dump the load in any direction.

Mini dumper

This tiny dumper is like a wheelbarrow with an engine. It can fit through doorways, into buildings, and gardens. It can even climb steps!

The operator steers using the handles.

Engine

Skip

Handles

The mini dumper can hold enough water to fill a bath.

Demolition excavator

Not every excavator helps to build things. Demolition excavators tear old buildings down!

Crusher

This high-reach excavator has an extra-long arm to reach the top of tall buildings.

Long boom

A powerful crusher jaw is attached to the arm. It tears off pieces of building and breaks them up.

Guard to protect cab from falling objects

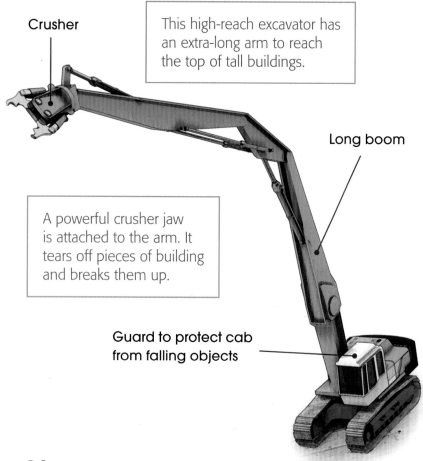

High tip dumper

This dumper can lift its skip high into the air before it tips. It can dump a load straight into a lorry or skip.

Look out for high tip dumpers on small building sites.

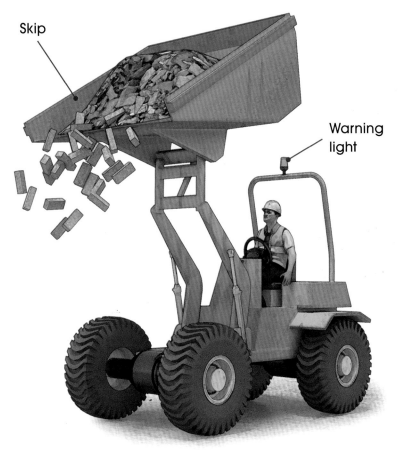

Skip

Warning light

Skid steer loader

This tiny loader steers like a vehicle with tracks. To steer left or right, the wheels on one side slow down.

Skid steer loaders can turn around on the spot.

Arms

Driver's cab

The driver climbs over the bucket to get into the cab.

Bucket

Articulated dump truck

Articulated dump trucks bend in the middle as they turn corners. This helps them to get around building sites.

Look for articulated dump trucks at roadworks. They deliver the materials used to build new roads.

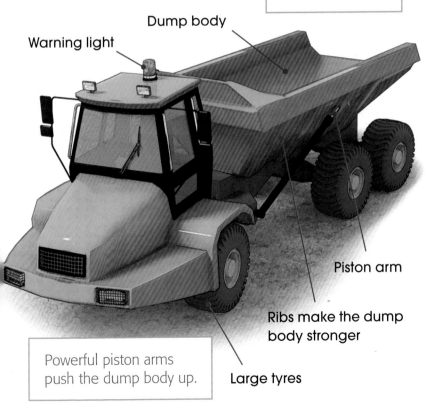

Dump body

Warning light

Piston arm

Ribs make the dump body stronger

Powerful piston arms push the dump body up.

Large tyres

Auger drill

Excavators dig very deep holes using drills called augers. An auger is like an enormous screw. As it turns, it cuts into the ground.

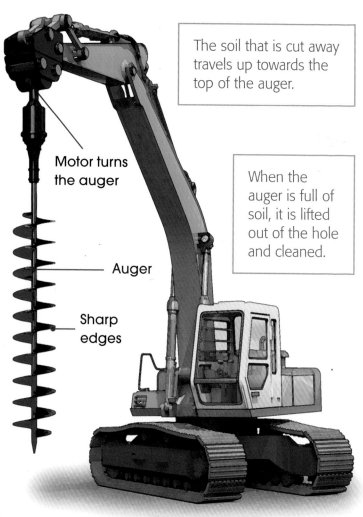

The soil that is cut away travels up towards the top of the auger.

Motor turns the auger

When the auger is full of soil, it is lifted out of the hole and cleaned.

Auger

Sharp edges

Heavy tipper truck

Big tipper trucks work just like small tipper trucks, but carry bigger loads. They deliver materials like sand and gravel to building sites.

This truck has 8 wheels to support heavy loads.

Dump body

Piston arm

Mass excavator

A building site excavator would fit in the bucket of this huge digger!

The bucket opens at the bottom to dump loads quickly.

Thick, heavy boom and arm

Bucket faces forwards

Enormous bucket

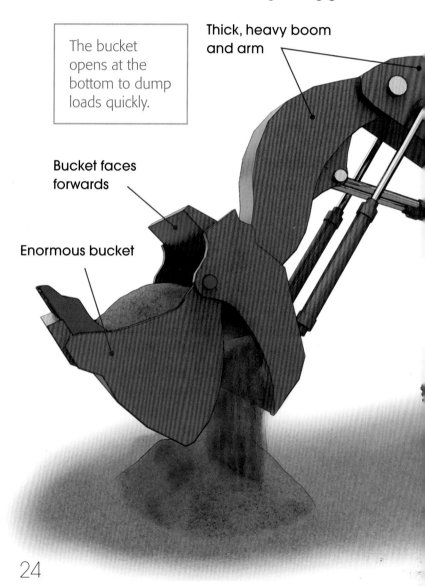

Mass excavators work at mines and quarries. They clear huge piles of rubble.

The operator climbs a ladder to get into the cab.

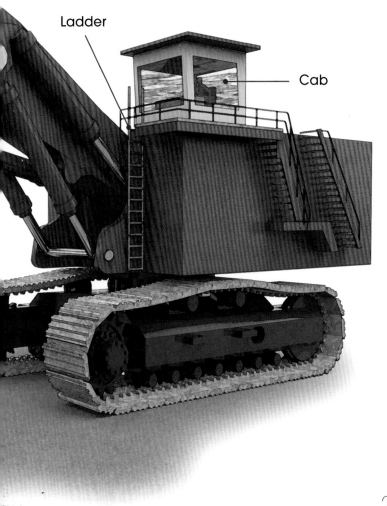

Ladder

Cab

Waste handler

This excavator works at a recycling plant. It uses a grab or grapple to sort through waste and find things that can be recycled.

Excavators with grabs and grapples are also used to clear sites before building starts.

Boom

Grab

Cab rises up to give operator a good view

Outrigger

Outrigger legs fold out from each side to spread the machine's weight and stop it from tipping over.

Wheels

Refuse compactor

This mighty machine works at a rubbish dump. Its job is to squash and squeeze rubbish so it takes up less space.

The giant dozer blade spreads out rubbish ready to be squashed.

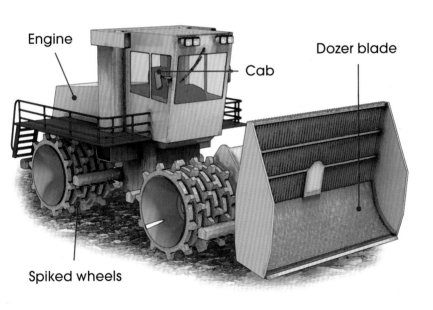

Engine

Cab

Dozer blade

Spiked wheels

Spiked wheels crush the rubbish and squeeze out any air.

Mini excavator

This excavator is small enough to drive into a house. It can work in tiny spaces, digging trenches for pipes and cables.

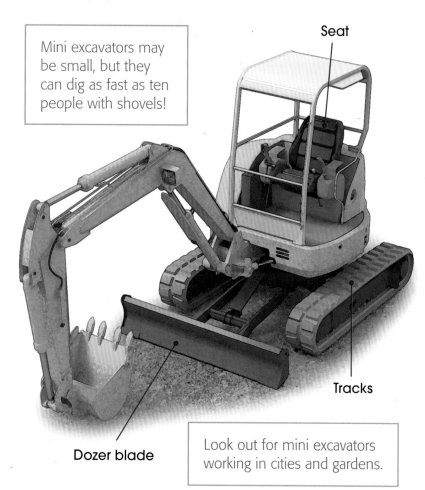

Mini excavators may be small, but they can dig as fast as ten people with shovels!

Seat

Tracks

Dozer blade

Look out for mini excavators working in cities and gardens.

Dragline excavator

This excavator is the size of a building. It is used in mines to move huge amounts of earth and rubble quickly.

Ropes drag the bucket across the ground and scoop up a load.

The boom swings around and dumps the load up to 200 metres away.

Huge boom

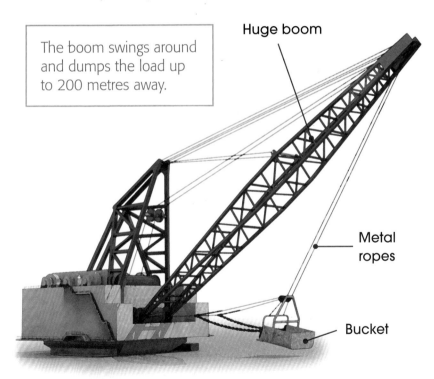

Metal ropes

Bucket

 # Tractor loader

Farmers need to move heavy loads of grain, animal food, and manure every day. Tractor loaders can get the job done.

Weights at the back stop the tractor tipping forwards as it picks up heavy loads.

Bucket

Loader arm

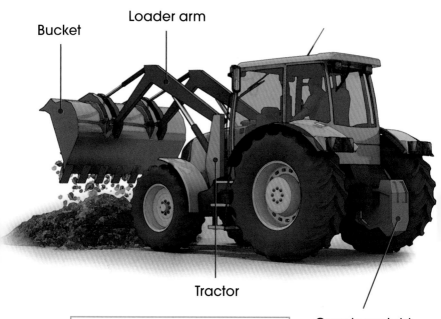

Tractor

Counterweight

The farmer can take the loader arms and bucket off, and use the tractor for other jobs.

Trencher

Builders have to dig long, straight trenches to lay pipes and cables. They can use special diggers called trenchers.

As the chain moves around, the teeth cut through the earth.

Chain

Trencher

Tough, steel tipped teeth

Semi-trailer dump truck

The trailer of this truck carries earth, rubble or stones over long distances.

The driver's cab and engine are in the tractor at the front.

Tractor

Carrying bigger
loads means fewer
trips are needed.

There are tipper
trailers that
dump the load
at the back, to
the side, and out
of the bottom.

Semi-trailer

Tractor wheels support some
of the trailer's weight

Lots of wheels
spread the weight
of the heavy load

Heavy hauler dump truck

The world's biggest dump trucks work at mines and quarries. They carry huge loads of heavy rocks.

The operator climbs a ladder to get into the cab.

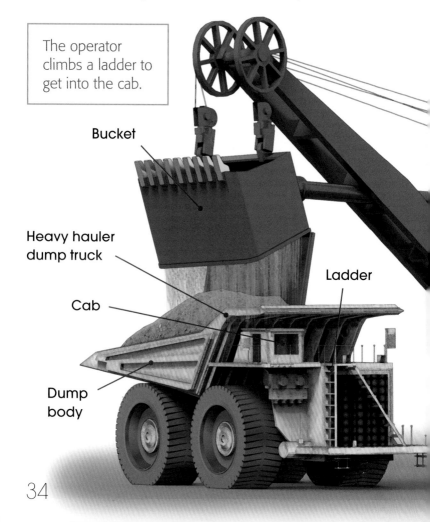

Bucket

Heavy hauler dump truck

Cab

Dump body

Ladder

Electric rope shovel

You can only spot these diggers at mines and quarries. They load rocks into huge dump trucks. Instead of having engines, they are powered by electricity.

Ropes pull the bucket through a pile of loose rock. The digger swings around to dump the load into the truck.

Metal ropes

Electric rope shovel

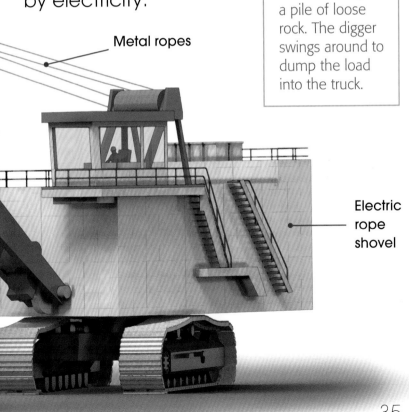

Transfer dump truck

This truck is a tipper truck that pulls a trailer with an extra load.

When the main dump body has been emptied, the second container slides into it. Now it can be tipped up too.

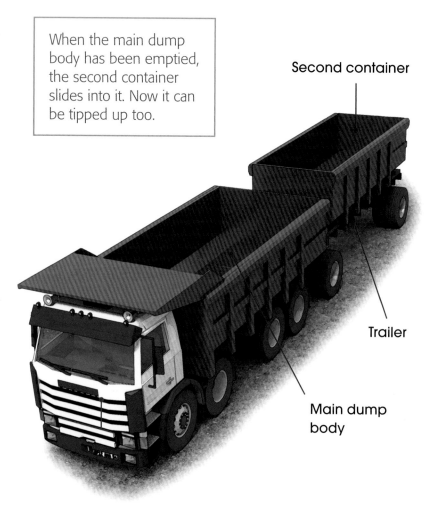

Second container

Trailer

Main dump body

Scraper

A scraper clears land ready to build a new road. Sharp blades scrape away earth and rubble, and collect it in a metal box called a bowl.

The scraper digs and loads, so it can work without other machines.

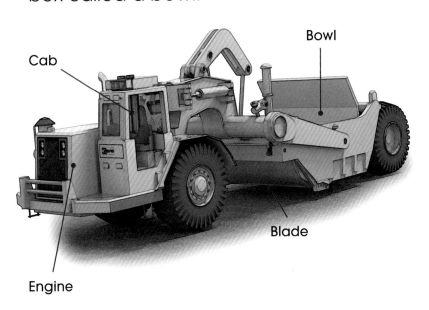

Bowl

Cab

Blade

Engine

Grader

New roads are built in layers. After each layer is added, it has to be flattened.

Exhaust pipe

Powerful engine

Curved blade

Six wheels

This is the grader's job. Its large blade scrapes along the ground, making it smooth and level.

The driver can raise, lower, and tilt the blade in any direction.

— Cab

Turntable

As the blade moves, anything in its way is flattened or pushed to the side.

Telehandler

A telehandler arm gets longer like a telescope. Different tools can be fitted on the end, to lift anything from a pile of rocks to a car.

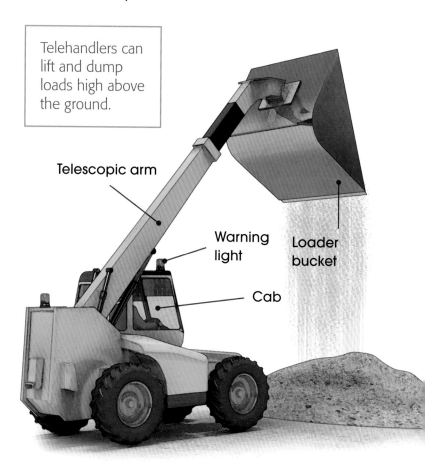

Telehandlers can lift and dump loads high above the ground.

Telescopic arm

Warning light

Loader bucket

Cab

Useful words

articulated a bendy vehicle with separate connected sections

boom a long moving arm

bucket a shovel for scooping up loads

cab the covered area where a driver or operator sits

construction building something

counterweight a heavy weight added to a machine to stop it tipping over as it lifts heavy loads

dump body the tipping skip or truck bed or a dumper or dump truck

engine a machine that burns fuel to power a vehicle

exhaust a pipe that carries heat and fumes away from an engine

outrigger a leg that folds out from the side of a machine to keep it steady, and take the weight off the wheels

piston arm a sliding arm that moves parts of a digger or dumper up and down

roll bar a strong metal bar that protects the driver if a machine rolls over

Spotter's guide

How many of these diggers
and dumpers have you seen?
Tick them when you spot them.

☐ Excavator
page 6

☐ Site dumper
page 8

☐ Rock breaker
page 9

☐ Bulldozer
page 10

Handheld breaker
page 11

Tipper truck
page 12

Loader
page 13

Backhoe loader
page 14

Tracked dumper
page 16

Mini dumper
page 17

Demolition
excavator
page 18

High tip
dumper
page 19

Skid steer loader
page 20

Articulated
dump truck
page 21

Auger drill
page 22

Heavy tipper
truck
page 23

44

Mass excavator
page 24

Waste handler
page 26

Refuse
compactor
page 27

Mini excavator
page 28

Dragline
excavator
page 29

Tractor loader
page 30

Trencher
page 31

Semi-trailer
dump truck
page 32

Heavy hauler
dump truck
page 34

Electric rope
shovel
page 35

Transfer dump
truck
page 36

Scraper
page 37

Grader
page 38

Telehandler
page 40

Find out more

If you would like to find out more about diggers and dumpers, you can visit some special sites in the UK. These websites are a good place to start.

JCB Explore
www.jcbexplore.com

JCB Factory Tours
www.jcb.co.uk/about/factory-tour

National Mining Museums
www.ncm.org.uk
www.museumwales.ac.uk/en/bigpit
www.scottishminingmuseum.com